FEDERAL ELECTION COMMISSION
999 E Street, N.W.
Washington, D.C. 20463

SENSITIVE

FIRST GENERAL COUNSEL'S REPORT

MUR: 6462
DATE COMPLAINT FILED: 3/16/2011
DATE OF NOTIFICATION: 3/23/2011
LAST RESPONSE RECEIVED: 10/19/2012
DATE ACTIVATED: 6/10/2011

EXPIRATION OF SOL: 1/16/2016 to 2/1/2017

COMPLAINANT:	Shawn Thompson
RESPONDENTS:	Donald J. Trump
	Michael Cohen
	Stewart Rahr
	The Trump Organization, LLC
	Should Trump Run Committee, Inc. f/k/a
	ShouldTrumpRun.com
RELEVANT STATUTES	2 U.S.C. § 431(2)
AND REGULATIONS:	2 U.S.C. § 431(8), (9)
	2 U.S.C. § 432(e)(1)
	2 U.S.C. § 433
	2 U.S.C. § 434
	2 U.S.C. § 441a
	2 U.S.C. § 441b
	11 C.F.R. § 100.72
	11 C.F.R. § 100.131
	11 C.F.R. § 101.1(a)
INTERNAL REPORTS CHECKED:	Disclosure Reports
OTHER AGENCIES CHECKED:	None

I.   INTRODUCTION

The Complaint in this matter alleges that Donald J. Trump violated the Federal Election

Campaign Act of 1971, as amended, (the "Act") while "testing the waters" for the 2012

presidential election. According to the Complaint, Trump accepted excessive or impermissible

1   contributions from The Trump Organization, LLC ("Trump LLC"), in connection with a

2   website, www.ShouldTrumpRun.com ("ShouldTrumpRun"), created by Trump LLC employee

3   Michael Cohen, and from Stewart Rahr, who paid for a flight Cohen took on Trump's privately

4   owned jet. The Complaint also alleges that ShouldTrumpRun is a political committee that has

5   failed to register with the Commission.

6   Respondents deny the allegations, noting that Trump publicly announced that he was not

7   a candidate for federal office. The Joint Response, submitted on behalf of all Respondents,

8   asserts that Cohen personally paid for the website and that the travel at issue was not in

9   connection with a federal election.[1]

10   Based on the available information, we recommend that the Commission find reason to

11   believe that Respondents violated the Commission regulations requiring "testing the waters"

12   activities to be paid for with hard money funds subject to the limitations and prohibitions in the

13   Act. Thus, we recommend that the Commission find reason to believe that Trump LLC, Cohen,

14   Rahr, and Should Trump Run[2] violated 11 C.F.R. § 100.131(a) by making in-kind

15   disbursements with impermissible funds, and that Trump violated 11 C.F.R. § 100.72(a) by

16   accepting the in-kind disbursements. We further recommend that the Commission find no

17   reason to believe that Trump violated 2 U.S.C. § 432(e)(1) or 11 C.F.R. § 101.1(a) by not fifihg

18   a Statement of Candidacy with the Commission designating a prinoipal campaign committee,

19   and find no reason to believe that that Trump, Trump LLC, Cohen, Rahr, or Should Trump Run

---

[1]   We provided Respondents with copies of the articles cited in this Report and in the proposed Factual and Legal Analysis. *See* Letter from Mark Allen, FEC, to Cleta Mitchell, Counsel (Oct. 5, 2012). In their response, Respondents reiterated their assertion that Trump was never a candidate for President. *See* Letter from Cleta Mitchell to Mark Allen (Oct. 19, 2012).

[2]   As discussed below, Should Trump Run Committee, Inc. registered with the Internal Revenue Service as a "Section 527" organization on September 1, 2011, with Cohen as its president, and appears to have merged with ShouldTrumpRun.

1   violated 2 U.S.C. §§ 441a or 441b by making excessive or impermissible contributions. In

2   addition, since any costs or payments associated with ShouldTrumpRun would likewise not be

3   considered contributions or expenditures, we recommend that the Commission find no reason to

4   believe Should Trump Run violated 2 U.S.C. §§ 433 or 434 by not registering and reporting as a

5   political committee.

6   **II.   FACTS**

7   Trump engaged in "testing the waters" activities during 2011 and early 2012 in

8   connection with a possible run for the Republican nomination for President and later for a

9   possible run as an independent. Trump ultimately decided not to run.[3]

10   Trump is the CEO of Trump LLC, a privately-owned conglomerate that owns, operates,

11 and develops hotels, resorts, and other properties. Trump LLC is owned and managed by the

12 Trump family. *See, e.g.,* http://www.trump.com (last visited Jan. 24, 2013). Cohen reportedly

13 serves as Executive Vice President of Trump LLC and Special Counsel to Trump.[4] Cohen and

---

[3]   *See, e.g.,* Huma Khan and Jennifer Winch, *Donald Trump Staff in Talks With Financiers, Campaign Managers to Explore Third Party Bid,* ABC NEWS, Jan. 30, 2012, *available at* http://abcnews.go.com/blogs/politics/2012/01/donald-trump-staff-reaching-out-to-financers-campaign-managers-to-explore-third-party-bid/ (last visited Jan. 24, 2013); Peter Woodifield, *Trump May Run as Independent in U.S. Presidential Election,* BLOOMBERG NEWS, June 20, 2011, *available at* http://www.bloomberg.com/news/print/2011-06-20/trump-may-run-as-independent-in-u-s-presidential-election-1-.html (last visited Jan. 24, 2013); From the Desk of Donald Trump: Why I cancelled the "great debate," (Dec. 13, 2011), http://www.youtube.com/watch?v=xLtPUXBcAZg&list=UU9AKA0PYiGCSPnfCEMaKtag&index=35&feature=plpp_video ("But the most important thing is I can't give up that possibility of running. I just feel like I owe it to myself, to my family, and perhaps most importantly to the country."); *Donald Trump Says His Interest in Presidential Run Is Not About Publicity,* ASSOCIATED PRESS, Mar. 9, 2011 *available at* http://cnsnews.com/news/article/donald-trump-says-his-interest-presidential-run-not-about-publicity (last visited Jan. 24, 2013); From the Desk of Donald Trump, 3/1/11, http://www.youtube.com/watch?v=B5Yc78ieF60&list=PLBB36D0C29844BEF8&index=14&feature=plpp_video ("So you'll have plenty of jobs if I decide to run and if I win.") (Mar. 1, 2011).

[4]   Cohen reportedly acknowledged that Trump is his "boss" and that they share a close working relationship; according to press reports, Cohen has an office on the same floor as Trump at the Trump LLC's Manhattan headquarters and stated that he sees Trump on a "daily" basis. *See, e.g.,* Michael Falcone, *Donald Trump's Political 'Pit Bull': Meet Michael Cohen,* ABC NEWS, Apr. 16, 2011, *available at* http://abcnews.go.com/Politics/donald-trumps-political-pit-bull-meet-michael-cohen/story?id=13386747 (last visited Jan. 24, 2013); Tom Beaumont, *Top Donald Trump Aide in Iowa Meeting with GOP Leaders,* DES MOINES

1   Rahr reportedly co-created the ShouldTrumpRun website,[5] which was initially used to poll

2   readers to gauge their support of Trump as a presidential candidate and later added a "Donate"

3   link allowing prospective contributors to donate up to $2,500 for the 2012 general election if

4   Trump decided to run.

5   According to the Complaint, in early 2011, Trump became a "de facto" candidate for the

6   Republican nomination for President. Compl. at 2. The Complaint asserts that, by employing

7   Cohen, the co-creator of ShouldTrunpRun, and giving him compensation, a telephone, and

8   office space, Trump LLC made an in-kind contribution to Trump's candidacy, in violation of

9   2 U.S.C. §§ 441a or 441b. Even if Trump never triggered candidate status under the Act, the

10   Complaint alleges that Respondents' "testing the waters" activities may have violated the "ban

11   on corporate" donations as well as the "limit of $2,500." Id. at 2. See 2 U.S.C. §§ 441b, 441a.[6]

12   The Response states that Trump "has never been a federal candidate and has further publicly

13   announced that he is not now and will not be a candidate for federal office in 2012." Resp. at 1.

14   A.   Cohen's Trip to Iowa

15   On March 7, 2011, Cohen flew to Iowa on Trump's privately owned jet. The Complaint

16   asserts that Cohen went to Iowa to campaign for Trump and that Rahr paid approximately

17   $125,000 for Cohen's flight.[7] Compl. at 2-3. The Complaint notes that Trump told the press on

---

REGISTER Blog, Mar. 7, 2011, *available at* http://blogs.desmoinesregister.com/dmr/index.php/2011/03/07/top-donald-trump-aide-in-iowa-meeting-with-gop-leaders (last visited Jan. 24, 2013) ("Beaumont Register article").

[5]   *See* Beaumont Register article.

[6]   Under the Act, for the 2012 election cycle, the individual contribution limit to a federal candidate is $2,500 per election. *See* 2 U.S.C. § 441a(a)(1)(A); http://www.fec.gov/pages/brochures/contriblimits.shtml.

[7]   Cohen reportedly stated that the flight was paid by Rahr. *See* Peter Hamby, *Trump Aide Grabs Attention in Iowa*, CNN POLITICS, Mar. 7, 2011, *available at* http://politicalticker.blogs.cnn.com/2011/03/07/trump-aide-grabs-attention-in-iowa (last visited Jan. 24, 2013).

1   March 10, 2011, "my representative was swamped by supporters when he went to Iowa."[8] *Id.*

2   Cohen reportedly flew to Iowa to meet with Republican party officials and, according to Cohen,

3   to "gaug[e] the reception I feel [Trump] would have when he comes to Iowa." *Top Aide Heads*

4   *to Iowa to Plug for a Possible Donald Trump Presidential Run in 2012,* NEW YORK DAILY

5   NEWS, Mar. 5, 2011 *available at* http://www.nydailynews.com/news/politics/top-aide-heads-

6   iowa-plug-donald-trump-presidential-run-2012-article-1.120758 (last visited Jan. 24, 2013).

7   A press release promoting the trip described Cohen as an employee of and counsel to Trump:

8   "Michael Cohen, Executive Vice President and Special Counsel to Donald J. Trump, will hold a

9   media availability at Signature FBO [Fixed Base Operator] in Des Moines tomorrow morning

10   [March 7, 2011] at 9:15 a.m." *See, e.g.,* Peter Hamby, *Trump Aide Grabs Attention in Iowa,*

11   CNN POLITICS, Mar. 7, 2011, *available at*

12   http://politicalticker.blogs.cnn.com/2011/03/07/trump-aide-grabs-attention-in-iowa (last visited

13   Jan. 24, 2013) ("Hamby CNN article").[9] According to the Complaint, Rahr's payment is a

---

[8]   Although the Complaint does not cite the publication quoting Trump, our news search revealed an
Associated Press report containing the following statement: "Trump says his representative was 'swamped' by
supporters when he went to Iowa." *Donald Trump Says His Interest in Presidential Run Is Not About Publicity,*
ASSOCIATED PRESS, Mar. 9, 2011 *available at* http://cnsnews.com/news/article/donald-trump-says-his-interest-
presidential-run-not-about-publicity (last visited Jan. 24, 2013).

[9]   In Cohen's role as a spokesman for Trump regarding potential campaign-related activities, in February
2011, Cohen reportedly met with the chairman of the Republican Party of Iowa at Trump headquarters in
Manhattan and then informed the press about a possible trip to Iowa by Trump to speak at a state Republican Party
fundraiser. Tom Beaumont, *Donald Trump Will Appear at Iowa Republican Dinner in June,* DES MOINES
REGISTER, Mar. 23, 2011. *See* Attach. 1. Upon arriving in Iowa two weeks later, Cohen appears to have met with
the same party official aboard Trump's jet to discuss Trump's potential candidacy. *See, e.g.,* Hamby CNN article.
When asked about Trump's comments about still considering a run for president, Cohen reportedly stated that
Trump's statement "speaks for itself and Mr. Trump has no additional comment at this time." Sheila Marikar and
Rick Klein, *Is Donald Trump Back in the 2012 Race?,* ABC NEWS blog, May 23, 2011, *available at*
http://blogs.abcnews.com/thenote/2011/05/is-donald-trump-back-in-the-2012-race.html (last visited Jan. 24, 2013).
Several months later, Cohen was reportedly still speaking on behalf of Trump's potential campaign-related
activities. In November 2011, Cohen reportedly stated "[Trump is] prepared to finance an independent run for
president if he's not satisfied with the Republican nominee," and that Trump will make a decision "in the first week
of June [2012]." Cohen added that "I already mapped out everything that has to be done to be an effective
candidate and what we'd have to do to get on the ballot on all 50 states." Neil King Jr., *Trump Threatens to Spend*
Millions on a Presidential Run, WALL STREET JOURNAL'S "Washington Wire," Nov. 22, 2011, *available at*
http://blogs.wsj.com/washwire/2011/11/22/trump-threatens-to-spend-millions-on-a-presidential-run/ (last visited

1   contribution to Trump and/or ShouldTrumpRun in excess of the Act's limitations. Compl.

2   at 2-3.

3   The Response does not provide any information as to the flight's purpose, how it was

4   paid for, or whether it cost $125,000 as alleged, but states that the Act's provisions "do not

5   extend to persons traveling for purposes not in connection with a federal candidate or

6   election."[10] Resp. at 1. The Response includes a chart labeled "Boeing 757-200 Jet" showing

7   that "the aircraft [referenced in the Complaint] is owned by entities whose sole 100% owner is

8   Donald J. Trump." *Id.* at 2. The Response asserts that even if Trump had become a federal

9   candidate, the Act specifically permits the unlimited use of an aircraft personally owned by a

10   candidate. *See id*; 2 U.S.C. § 439a(c)(3)(A).

11   **B.   ShouldTrumpRun.com**

12   The Complaint alleges that ShouldTrumpRun is a political committee that failed to

13   register with the Commission as required by the Act. The Complaint alleges that the website

14   "actively" promotes Trump's candidacy because it states in large type, superimposed over a

15   photo of the White House, "We're Drafting Supporters in Iowa & New Hampshire," and "offers

16   an interface where supporters can provide their contact Information, and state [of residence]."

17   Compl. at 3-4. The Complaint notes that the website displays a "Join the Movement" banner

---

Jan. 24, 2013). ShouldTrumpRun also posted this article at http://shouldtrumprun.com/node/155 (last visited Jan. 24, 2013).

[10]   Cohen reportedly stated that the flight was paid by Stewart Rahr, whom Cohen identified as the co-creator of ShouldTrumpRun, and not with any of Trump's money. *See* Hamby CNN Article; Beaumont Register article; *Donald Trump's Political 'Pit Bull': Meet Michael Cohen*, ABC NEWS, Apr. 16, 2011, *available at* http://abcnews.go.com/Politics/donald-trumps-political-pit-bull-meet-michael-cohen/story?id=13386747 (last visited Jan. 24, 2013). Cohen reportedly further stated that "my trip was not for Mr. Trump but rather as co-creator of ShouldTrumpRun.com," noting that the website is paid for by Rahr and himself. Cohen described his Iowa trip as a "personal day" and stated that he would "report back to Mr. Trump when he hopefully decides to ren in June." James Q. Lynch, *Trump Employee: U.S. Needs His Boss 'More than Ever'*, SIOUX CITY JOURNAL, Mar. 7, 2011, *available at* http://siouxcityjournal.com/news/local/trump-nmployee-u-s-needs-his-boss-more-than-ever/article_25045990-5511-5afe-804d-c901b5d01113.html (last visited Jan. 24, 2013). The Response does not address the alleged cost of the flight and it is not clear how the Complaint arrived at the cost figure of $125,000.

1 and contains links using such phrases as "Donald Trump on the record about running for

2 president." *Id.* at 4. The Complaint asserts that the only purpose of such information is to use it

3 to support Trump's candidacy. It alleges that the website "also contains videos of Trump, made

4 especially for the website, taped in Trump's office" at Trump LLC headquarters. *Id.* The

5 Complaint concludes that Trump is a candidate because he "authorized the actions" of Cohen

6 and ShouldTrumpRun, and "promoted the same in the national media." Compl. at 4. The

7 Response states that Cohen personally paid for the ShouldTrumpRun website and thus, it

8 "constitutes no expenditure in connection with a federal candidate." Resp. at 1.

9   The Complaint also focuses on a "poll" conducted by ShouldTrumpRun. *See*

10 http://shouldtrumprun.com/node/142 (last visited Jan. 24, 2013). It appears that, at the time of

11 the filing of the Complaint in March 2011 through approximately July 2011, the home page of

12 the website posed the poll question "Should Donald Trump enter the 2012 presidential race?"

13 *See* Attach. 2 at 4. A tally of the results of the poll, which is now closed, was presented on the

14 home page immediately below the poll question. *Id.* The website included two other questions,

15 "Would you vote for Donald Trump in 2012?" and "Who would you favor in the 2012

16 Presidential Election?" *Id.* at 4-5. In connection with the latter question, the website permits

17 two possible answers, "Donald J. Trump" or "Barack Obama." *Id.* The website also posted an

18 entry titled "From Donald Trump...," containing a "Tweet" from Trump: "Thanks for all of

19 your tremendous support over the past few months, stay tuned!" *Id.* at 2. The home page

20 contained the following disclaimer: "This site is not endorsed by Donald J. Trump." *Id.* at 6.

21   In May 2011, Trump publicly announced that he would not seek the 2012 Republican

22 nomination for U.S. President. *See* Resp. at 1. But, according to press accounts, Trump later

1   stated that he was considering running for President as an independent, and he continued to

2   express such an interest for several months into early 2012.[11]

3   During this period, on September 1, 2011, the Should Trump Run Committee, Inc.

4   registered with the Internal Revenue Service ("IRS") as a Section 527 organization with Cohen

5   as its president. This organization described its purpose as "To explore the

6   possibility/determine support and solicit funds to draft Donald J. Trump to run for President of

7   the United States."[12] See Attach. 3. Around the same time, ShouldTrumpRun posted the

8   following disclaimer at the bottom of each page of the website: "Paid for by Should Trump

9   Run Committee, Inc. Not authorized by any candidate or candidate's committee." And on the

10   home page ShouldTrumpRun included the statement: "Site is owned by Should Trump Run

11   Committee, Inc." See Attach. 3. ShouldTrumpRun posted a press account on September 2,

12   2011 stating that "Trump's top political operative, Michael Cohen, who founded the website,

13   ShouldTrumpRun.com has morphed it into a so-called 527 group which is allowed to raise

14   money for political activities and issue advocacy." See Michael Falcone and Jennifer Wlach,

---

[11]   See, e.g., Peter Woodifield, *Trump May Run as Independent in U.S. Presidential Election*, BLOOMBERG NEWS, June 20, 2011, *available at* http://www.bloomberg.com/news/print/2011-06-20/trump-may-run-as-independent-in-u-s-presidential-election-1-.html (last visited Jan. 24, 2013); CNN Transcripts, *Trump On Downgrade*, CNN NEWSROOM, Aug. 8, 2011, *available at* http://archives.cnn.com/TRANSCRIPTS/1108/08/cnr.04.html (last visited Jan. 24, 2013) ("...I was happy with the decision [not to run], but if the economy continues to be bad, and it looks to me like it's getting worse and not better, and if the Republicans pick the wrong person, I would seriously consider doing it as an independent..."); Sarah Maslin Nir, *Trump Quits G.O.P.*, NEW YORK TIMES, Dec. 24, 2011, *available at* http://thecaucus.blogs.nytimes.com/2011/12/24/trump-quits-g-o-p/ (last visited Jan. 24, 2013) (reporting that Cohen confirmed that Trump withdrew from the Republican Party to retain the ability to run as an independent candidate in the 2012 presidential election); Huma Khan and Jennifer Wlach, *Donald Trump Staff in Talks With Financiers, Campaign Managers to Explore Third Party Bid*, ABC NEWS, Jan. 30, 2012, *available at* http://abcnews.go.com/blogs/politics/2012/01/donald-trump-staff-reaching-out-to-financers-campaign-managers-to-explore-third-party-bid/ (last visited Jan. 24, 2013). Trump reportedly endorsed Mitt Romney for President on February 2, 2012. *See* Ashley Parker and Trip Gabriel, *Trump Endorses Romney in a 7-Minute Appearance*, NEW YORK TIMES, Feb. 2, 2012, *available at* http://thecaucus.blogs.nytimes.com/2012/02/02/confusion-over-trump-endorses-romney/ (last visited Jan. 24, 2013).

[12]   Should Trump Run Committee, Inc. registered as a domestic nonprofit corporation with the Secretary of State of California on September 7, 2011.

1 *Pro-Donald Trump Website Evolves Into 527 Group,* ABC NEWS, Sept. 2, 2011, *available at*

2 http://www.shouldtrumprun.com/content/pro-donald-trump-website-evolves-527-group (last

3 visited Jan. 24, 2013) ("Falcone and Wlach ABC article").

4   ShouldTrumpRun also added a "Donate" link to the home page of the website in

5 approximately mid-September 2011; clicking on the link brought up a solicitation page stating

6 that "[o]ur goal is to encourage Mr. Trump – who is NOT presently a candidate – to become

7 one, and to explore the potential support for his possible candidacy," and contains an online

8 form requesting donations from website visitors.[13] *See* Attach. 4 at 1, 8, and 11. A prospective

9 contributor could make contributions in various amounts up to $2,500, but the form also

10 included a blank space in which any amount could be entered. In order to make a contribution,

11 the prospective contributor was required to "affirm," *inter alia,* that the following statement was

12 "true and accurate": "I agree that if Mr. Trump does run, the first $2,500 of my contribution

13 shall then be designated for the 2012 general election. Any donation in excess of $2,500 must

14 either be refunded or redesignated [sic] to a spouse." *Id.* The solicitation page contains

15 cautionary language about corporate/union/reimbursed funds not being accepted, and states that

16 name/occupation/employer/address information is "[r]equired by federal law." *Id.* Should

17 Trump Run Committee, Inc. has not registered as a political committee with the Commission

18 and has not filed any disclosure reports with the IRS as a 527 organization.

19   ShouldTrumpRun removed the "Donate" link in approximately February 2012. In

20 March 2012, ShouldTrumpRun renamed itself TRUMPHQ.com, but remains accessible at

21 www.shouldtrumprun.com. The website was modified to include the statement, "We fully

22 respect Mr. Trump's decision to endorse Mitt Romney, but firmly believe that we need Trump

---

[13]   Cohen reportedly stated that the Section 527 organization would continue to promote the principles and issues that Trump espouses and predicted that it would "raise an enormous amount of money right away." *See* Falcone and Wlach ABC article.

1   in DC," and a poll entitled "Donald Trump would be the best" that offered the choices of

2   "President," "Vice President," "Secretary of State," "Secretary of Defense" and "Secretary of

3   Commerce." *See* Attach. 5. The website also added disclaimers stating that "TrumpHQ.com is

4   not associated with Donald J. Trump," and that it is "[n]ot authorized by any candidate or

5   candidate's committee." *Id.*

6   **III.   LEGAL ANALYSIS**

7   An individual is deemed to be a "candidate" for purposes of the Act if he or she receives

8   contributions or makes expenditures in excess of $5,000, or if the individual "has given his or

9   her consent to another person to receive contributions or make expenditures on behalf of such

10   individual and if such person has received such contributions" or has made such expenditures in

11   excess of $5,000. 2 U.S.C. § 431(2)(A), (B). Once an individual meets the $5,000 threshold,

12   the candidate has 15 days to designate a principal campaign committee by filing a Statement of

13   Candidacy with the Commission. 2 U.S.C. § 432(e)(1); 11 C.F.R. § 101.1(a). The principal

14   campaign committee must file a Statement of Organization within ten days of its designation,

15   *see* 2 U.S.C. § 433(a), and must file disclosure reports with the Commission in accordance with

16   2 U.S.C. § 434(a) and (b).

17   The Commission has established limited exemptions from these thresholds, which

18   permit an individual to test the feasibility of a campaign for federal office without becoming a

19   candidate under the Act. Commonly referred to as the "testing the waters" exemptions,

20   11 C.F.R. §§ 100.72 and 100.131, respectively, exclude from the definitions of "contribution"

21   and "expenditure" those funds received and payments made solely to determine whether an

22   individual should become a candidate.[14] *See* 2 U.S.C. § 431(8), (9). Such "funds received" and

---

[14]   The Commission has emphasized the narrow scope of these exemptions to the Act's disclosure
requirements. *See Explanation and Justification for Regulations on Payments Received for Testing the Waters*

1 "payments made" include in-kind gifts of anything of value. *See* Advisory Op. 1981-32

2 (Askew). "Testing the waters" activities include, but are not limited to, payments for polling,

3 telephone calls, and travel. 11 C.F.R. §§ 100.72(a), 100.131(a). An individual who is "testing

4 the waters" need not register or file disclosure reports with the Commission unless and until the

5 individual subsequently decides to run for Federal office. *See id.*; Advisory Op. 1979-26

6 (Grassley). Only hard money funds subject to the prohibitions and limitations in the Act may

7 be used for "testing the waters" activities. 11 C.F.R. §§ 100.72(a), 100.131(a).[15]

8   Once an individual begins to campaign or decides to become a candidate, funds that

9 were raised or spent to "test the waters" apply to the $5,000 threshold for qualifying as a

10 candidate. 11 C.F.R. §§ 100.72(a), 100.131(a). Once an individual has become a candidate, is

11 no longer "testing the waters," and has raised or spent more than $5,000, he or she must register

12 as a candidate with the Commission.

13   Commission regulations set out a non-exhaustive list of activities that indicate that an

14 individual is no longer testing the waters and has decided to become a candidate. Such indicia

15 include (1) using general public political advertising to publicize his or her intention to

16 campaign for Federal office; (2) raising funds in excess of what could reasonably be expected to

17 be used for exploratory activities or undertaking activity designed to amass campaign funds that

---

Activities, 50 Fed. Reg. 9992, 9993 (Mar. 13, 1985) ("*Testing the Waters E&J*") ("The Commission has, therefore, amended the rules to ensure that the 'testing the waters' exemptions will not be extended beyond their original purpose. Specifically, these provisions are intended to be limited exemptions from the reporting requirements of the Act . . . .").

[15]   The Commission's regulations previously permitted individuals to accept funds in excess of the limits at 2 U.S.C. § 441a(a) and funds from prohibited sources for "testing the waters" activities, but required that the individual repay or refund any excessive or prohibited contributions received during the "testing the waters" period within ten days after becoming a candidate. In 1985 the Commission amended the regulations to require that all funds received for "testing the waters" be subject to the Act's limitations and prohibitions. In its Explanation and Justification, the Commission stated that it "views the amended regulations as reducing the potential for circumvention of the prohibitions and limitations of the Act. These revisions also ensure consistent application of the Act's contribution limitations and prohibitions." *Testing the Waters E&J*, 50 Fed. Reg. at 9994.

1   would be spent after he or she becomes a candidate; (3) making or authorizing written or oral

2   statements that refer to him or her as a candidate for a particular office; (4) conducting activities

3   in close proximity to the election or over a protracted period of time; and (5) taking action to

4   qualify for the ballot under state law. 11 C.F.R. §§ 100.72(b), 100.131(b). These regulations

5   seek to draw a distinction between activities directed to an evaluation of the feasibility of one's

6   candidacy and conduct or statements signifying that a decision to become a candidate has been

7   made. *See, e.g.*, Advisory Op. 1981-32 (Askew).

8   **A.   Trump's Candidate Status**

9   The Complaint alleges that Trump became a candidate but never filed a Statement of

10   Candidacy. Compl. at 2. The available information does not indicate that Trump made any

11   statements referring to himself as a candidate or indicating that he made a decision to run for

12   any federal office. The statements attributed to Trump on the ShouldTrumpRun website are

13   couched in terms of Trump *considering* whether to run for President.[16] In numerous videos that

14   were posted on the website (most appear to be links to short clips on the "Trump Channel" on

15   YouTube, *see* http://www.youtube.com/user/trump), Trump consistently frames his candidacy

16   in *potential* terms.[17] These statements about a potential candidacy do not establish that Trump

17   had decided to become a candidate.[18] The solicitation page brought up by ShouldTrumpRun's

---

[16]   *See, e.g.*, http://www.trumphq.com/content/cnn-donald-trump-considers-presidential-run-2012 ("Donald Trump tells CNN's Wolf Blitzer he's giving 'very serious thought' to running for President in 2012.") (Jan. 14, 2011); http://trumphq.com/content/donald-trump-seriously-considering-running-president-2012 ("Donald Trump said today he's 'seriously' considering running for the presidency in 2012.") (Oct. 5, 2010).

[17]   *See, e.g.*, http://www.youtube.com/watch?v=xLtPUXBcAZg&list=UU9AKA0PYiGCSPqfCEMaKtag&index=35&feature=plpp_video ("But the most important thing is I can't give up that possibility of running. I just feel like I owe it to myself, to my family, and perhaps most importantly the country.") (Dec. 13, 2011); http://www.youtube.com/watch?v=B5Yc78ieF60&list=PLBB36D0C29844BEF8&index=14&feature=plppvideo ("So you'll have plenty of jobs if I decide to run and if I win.") (Mar. 1, 2011).

[18]   *See, e.g.*, MUR 6330 (Johnson) (Commission found no reason to believe that Johnson became a candidate where pages from his exploratory committee's website included the statements "as I consider a run," and "many

1   "Donate" link similarly expresses Trump's candidacy in potential terms. The top of the

2   solicitation page states "[o]ur goal is to encourage Mr. Trump – *who is NOT presently a*

3   *candidate* – to become one, and to explore the potential support for his possible candidacy."

4   *See* Attach. 4 at 8 (emphasis added). The solicitation further reads "I agree that *if Mr. Trump*

5   *does run*, the first $2,500 of my contribution shall then be designated for the 2012 general

6   election." *See id.* at 11 (emphasis added).[19]

7   In sum, Respondents' activity appears to have been confined to "testing the waters."

8   Accordingly, we recommend that the Commission find no reason to believe that Trump violated

9   2 U.S.C. § 432(e)(1) or 11 C.F.R. § 101.1(a) by failing to file a Statement of Candidacy with the

10   Commission designating a principal campaign committee. In addition, because Trump was not

11   a candidate, none of the alleged activities would be contributions or expenditures; thus, we also

12   recommend that the Commission find no reason to believe that that Trump, Rahr, Trump LLC,

13   Cohen, or ShouldTrumpRun violated 2 U.S.C. §§ 441a or 441b by making excessive or

14   impermissible contributions. In addition, since any costs or payments associated with

15   ShouldTrumpRun would likewise not be considered contributions or expenditures, we

16   recommend that the Commission find no reason to believe ShouldTrumpRun violated 2 U.S.C.

17   §§ 433 or 434 by not registering and reporting as a political committee.

---

have encouraged me to run for office" and a biographical packet entitled "Get to Know Bill Johnson" contained an introduction stating that Johnson was "humbled and honored that folks are encouraging him to run for public office.").

[19]   We do not know how much ShouldTrumpRun raised, as it never registered and reported with the Commission and it never filed a disclosure report with the IRS. Even assuming that ShouldTrumpRun raised over $5,000, the Act's candidate threshold, and Trump consented to ShouldTrumpRun raising the funds on his behalf, *see* 2 U.S.C. § 431(2)(B), the Commission has found that exceeding this $5,000 threshold, or even raising a more significant amount of funds for exploratory activities, is not sufficient by itself to convert a potential candidate and his or her activities from "testing the waters" into candidate status. *See, e.g.,* MUR 6224 (Fiorina) (finding no reason to believe where a Senate candidate's campaign committee raised in excess of $600,000 in contributions during the "testing the waters" phase of a campaign); MUR 5934 (Thompson) (dismissing complaint where a Presidential candidate's campaign committee raised over $9 million and spent less than $3 million prior to announcement of candidacy).

1   **B.   Impermissible Funds for Testing the Waters Activity**

2   Regardless of whether Trump triggered candidate status under the Act, the Complaint

3   alleges that Respondents' "testing the waters" activities may have violated the "ban on

4 . corporate" donations as well as the "limit of $2,500." Compl. at 2.

5   Based on the available information, it appears that Trump may have directed, or

6   otherwise been sufficiently involved in, the alleged activities such that payments made by other

7   Respondents for these activities should be considered in-kind disbursements accepted by

8   Trump. Since the disbursements may have been made from possibly prohibited sources (the

9   Trump Organization) or in amounts in excess of the $2,500 individual contribution limitation

10   (Stewart Rahr), Trump may have accepted impermissible in-kind disbursements to fund his

11   "testing the waters" activities. *See* 11 C.F.R. §§ 100.72(a), 100.131(a) (only funds permissible

12   under the Act may be used for "testing the waters" activities).

13   The Commission has concluded that "testing the waters" activities must comport with

14   the limitations and prohibitions in the Act. *See supra* n.15 and accompanying text.   In

15   MUR 5722 (Lauzen), for example, the Complaint alleged that a potential candidate used funds

16   from his state re-election committee to pay for an exploratory telephone poll for a possible run

17   for Congress. The Commission concluded that the state committee violated 11 C.F.R.

18   § 100.131(a) by making an in-kind disbursement, by conducting the poll for "testing the waters"

19   purposes, and that the potential candidate violated 11 C.F.R. § 100.72(a) by accepting the in-

20   kind disbursement. *See* MUR 5722 Factual and Legal Analysis.[20]   Similarly, in MUR 2133

21   (Bush), the Republican National Committee ("RNC") made a $17,610 in-kind "testing the

---

[20]   The Commission dismissed the allegation with an admonishment, based on (1) the small amount of the in-kind disbursement ($4,250), (2) the fact that the individual had not and may never have become a candidate for federal office, and (3) information suggesting that he had done nothing else to "test the waters" or further a potential candidacy for federal office.

1   waters" disbursement for a poll for then Vice President George H.W. Bush, who at the time was

2   considering a run for President, which exceeded the limit at 2 U.S.C. § 441a(a)(2)(A) by

3    $12,610. The Commission found reason to believe the RNC violated the "testing the waters"

4   provisions by making an excessive in-kind disbursement to then Vice President Bush in the

5   form of poll results, and that he violated the provisions by accepting the in-kind disbursement.[21]

6   *See also* Advisory Op. 1998-18 (Washington State Democratic Committee) (deciding that the

7   costs of a telephone poll conducted for the purpose of "testing the waters" for a potential federal

8   candidate, who never became a candidate, must be funded from the State party's federal

9   account).

10   As noted above, the Complaint alleges that Cohen used Trump's private jet to fly to

11   Iowa to campaign for Trump, that Rahr paid $125,000 to cover the cost of the flight, and that

12   Trump stated that his representative was swamped by supporters when he went to Iowa.

13   Compl. at 2-3. The Response does not address these allegations; rather, it asserts that the flight

14   was not candidate- or election-related and, even if it were related, the use of the aircraft would

15   be exempt from the payment and reimbursement requirements at 2 U.S.C. § 439a(c)(3)(A).

16   We disagree. There is reason to believe that the flight to Iowa may have resulted in an

17   in-kind disbursement accepted by Trump, because the available information suggests that

---

[21]   After Vice President Bush became a candidate for President, the Commission pursued his authorized campaign committee, George Bush for President, Inc., which was his "successor in interest" in the proceedings. The Commission found probable cause to believe George Bush for President, Inc. violated 11 C.F.R. § 100.7(b)(1) by accepting an in-kind disbursement for "testing the waters" from the RNC in excess of the Act's limits. The matter was settled through a conciliation agreement that did not require payment of a civil penalty; the relevant provision stated "Respondent [Bush Committee] will conciliate this matter on the basis that it will pay MOR [the polling vendor] $17,610. This expenditure will be reported by Respondent and will count towards the overall spending limit. Because this payment is $5,000 more than the amount the Commission has treated as impermissibly received by Respondent, no civil penalty will be paid by Respondent." The Commission found no probable cause to believe that Vice President Bush personally violated 11 C.F.R. § 100.7(b)(1) and took no further action with respect to the violation of 11 C.F.R. § 100.8(b)(1) by the RNC. (The "testing the waters" provisions located at 11 C.F.R. §§ 100.7(b)(1) and 100.8(b)(1) were redesignated 11 C.F.R. §§ 100.72(a) and 100.131(a) in a restructuring of the Commission's regulations that followed the enactment of the Bipartisan Campaign Reform Act of 2002 (BCRA), Pub. L. No. 107-155.)

1 Trump was involved in activity (whether Trump directed Cohen to travel to Iowa, permitted the

2 use of his jet by Cohen, or otherwise discussed the trip with Cohen) that involved "testing the

3 waters." *See* Advisory Op. 1985-40 (Republican Majority Fund) (finding travel costs of

4 associates of potential candidate to attend events as potential candidate's representatives are

5 "testing the waters").[22] Because Rahr could have permissibly contributed only $2,500 to Trump

6 were Trump a candidate, the remaining amount ($122,500) would have constituted an excessive

7 in-kind disbursement. *See* 2 U.S.C. § 441a(a)(1)(A); 11 C.F.R. § 100.131(a).

8   The Complaint further asserts that, by employing Cohen, the Trump Organization made

9 a prohibited or excessive in-kind contribution to Trump's candidacy. Compl. at 3. The Act

10 defines contributions to include paying "compensation for the personal services of another

11 person which are rendered to a political committee without charge for any purpose," except for

12 legal and accounting services as described at 2 U.S.C. § 431(8)(B)(viii). 2 U.S.C.

13 § 431(8)(A)(ii). *See also* 11 C.F.R. §§ 100.54, 100.74, and 100.75.

14   The allegations concerning Cohen are not addressed in the Response; no information is

15 included about him other than that he "personally" paid for the ShouldTrumpRun website. *See*

16 Resp. at 1. The available information suggests that Cohen may have engaged in "testing the

17 waters" activities at the direction of Trump and as part of his work duties with the Trump

18 Organization. Cohen described his Iowa trip as a "personal day," but that he would "report

19 back" to his "boss" Trump; other information suggests that Cohen may have been engaging in

20 similar activities at his workplace at the Trump Organization, for example, meeting with a

---

[22]   Although there is no information that Trump had a formal campaign organization in place at the time of Cohen's Iowa trip, the alleged payment by Rahr for the flight is akin to a provision of goods or services to a campaign that the Commission has generally considered to be a direct in-kind contribution made by a third party and accepted by a federal committee. *See, e.g.,* MUR 5366 (Edwards) (conciliation agreement with presidential campaign committee described acceptance of prohibited in-kind contributions that included, *inter alia*, payment by incorporated law firm for hotel and car rental expenses of committee employees).

1   Republican party official. *See, e.g.*, James Q. Lynch, *Trump Employee: U.S. Needs His Boss*

2   *'More than Ever'*, SIOUX CITY JOURNAL, Mar. 7, 2011, *available at*

3   http://siouxcityjournal.com/news/local/trump-employee-u-s-needs-his-boss-more-than-

4   ever/article_25045990-5511-5afe-804d-c901b5d01113.html (last visited Jan. 24, 2013); Tom

5   Beaumont, *Donald Trump Will Appear at Iowa Republican Dinner in June*, DES MOINES

6   REGISTER, Mar. 23, 2011 (Attach. 1). If Cohen was conducting these activities as Trump's

7   employee, the Trump Organization would have made an in-kind disbursement to Trump using

8   federally impermissible funds. *See* 2 U.S.C. §§ 441a, 441b; 11 C.F.R. § 100.131(a).[23]

9   The Complaint further alleges that Cohen directs the activities of ShouldTrumpRun, that

10   Trump "authorized" the "actions" of Cohen and ShouldTrumpRun, and that the website

11   "contains videos of Trump, made especially for the website, taped in Trump's office" at the

12   the Trump Organization. Compl. at 4. Other than stating that Cohen paid for the website, the

13   Response also fails to address these allegations.

14   As noted, a "contribution" includes a payment by one person to another person for

15   personal services provided by that other person to a political committee without charge for any

16   purpose; conversely, the Act provides that "the value of services provided *without*

17   *compensation* by any individual who *volunteers* on behalf of a candidate or political committee"

18   is *not* a "contribution." 2 U.S.C. § 431(8)(B)(i) (emphasis added). The Commission's

19   regulations exempt volunteer internet activity, when undertaken by an individual without

20   compensation, from the definition of "contribution," even where an individual or group of

21   individuals coordinates with the candidate. 11 C.F.R. § 100.94. If Cohen were operating and

22   paying for the website at the direction of Trump and as part of his employment, he would not

---

[23]   The amount at issue would depend on, for example, the time Cohen spent on these activities and the value of any resources used; the permissibility of the source would depend on whether the Trump Organization, a limited liability company, is treated as a partnership or a corporation under the Act. *See* 11 C.F.R. § 110.1(g).

1   qualify for the volunteer exemption, and thus Cohen and ShouldTrumpRun would have made an

2   in-kind disbursement of federally impermissible funds. *See* 11 C.F.R. § 100.131(a).

3   The available information indicates that Trump may have been sufficiently involved in

4   the alleged "testing the waters" activities such that they should be considered in-kind

5   disbursements accepted by Trump; further, the activities may not have been paid for with

6   "funds permissible under the Act." *See* 11 C.F.R. §§ 100.72(a), 100.131(a). Therefore, we

7   recommend that the Commission find reason to believe that Rahr, Trump LLC, Cohen, and

8   ShouldTrumpRun violated 11 C.F.R. § 100.131(a), and that Donald J. Trump violated 11 C.F.R.

9   § 100.72(a).

10   **IV.   PROPOSED INVESTIGATION**

11   An investigation to determine whether the disbursements at issue were accepted by

12   Trump would focus primarily on whether Trump directed or approved Cohen's trip to Iowa and

13   the use of Trump's jet and whether Trump was involved with other alleged activities of Cohen,

14   including operating the website ShouldTrumpRun.com. We would also seek information about

15   Rahr's alleged $125,000 payment for Trump's jet, including any related discussions Rahr may

16   have had with Cohen or Trump. We expect to request contemporaneous documents and

17   communications regarding these activities including documents relating to the formation of

18   Should Trump Run Committee, Inc., the Section 527 organization. Although we would first

19   seek information voluntarily from Respondents, we recommend that the Commission authorize

20   the use of compulsory process, including the issuance of appropriate interrogatories, document

21   subpoenas, and deposition subpoenas, as necessary.

1 **V.   RECOMMENDATIONS**

2   1. Find reason to believe that Stewart Rahr, The Trump Organization, LLC, Michael
3   Cohen, and Should Trump Run Committee, Inc. f/k/a ShouldTrumpRun.com
4   violated 11 C.F.R. § 100.131(a).
5
6   2. Find reason to believe that Donald J. Trump violated 11 C.F.R. § 100.72(a).
7
8   3. Find no reason to believe that Donald J. Trump violated 2 U.S.C. § 432(e)(1) or
9   11 C.F.R. § 101.1(a).
10
11   4. Find no reason to believe that Donald J. Trump, Michael Cohen, Stewart Rahr, The
12   Trump Organization, LLC, or Should Trump Run Committee, Inc. f/k/a
13   ShouldTrumpRun.com violated 2 U.S.C. §§ 441a or 441b.
14
15   5. Find no reason to believe that Should Trump Run Committee, Inc. f/k/a
16   ShouldTrumpRun.com violated 2 U.S.C. §§ 433 or 434.
17
18   6. Authorize the use of compulsory process, as necessary.
19
20   7. Approve the attached Factual and Legal Analysis.
21
22   8. Approve the appropriate letters.
23
24   Anthony Herman
25   General Counsel
26
27   Daniel A. Petalas
28   Associate General Counsel for Enforcement
29
30
31 Date: 1-25-13   Kathleen M. Guith
32   Kathleen M. Guith
33   Deputy Associate General Counsel
34   for Enforcement
35
36
37
38   Peter G. Blumberg
39   Assistant General Counsel
40
41
42
43   Mark Allen
44   Attorney
45

1   Attachments:
2   1. Tom Beaumont, *Donald Trump Will Appear at Iowa Republican Dinner in June*, DES
3   MOINES REGISTER, Mar. 23, 2011
4   2. Home Page of www.ShouldTrumpRun.com (dated June 20, 2011)
5   3. ShouldTrumpRun IRS Section 527 Registration Form
6   4. ShouldTrumpRun.com September 2011 website with solicitation form
7   5. www.ShouldTrumpRun.com revised March 2012
8

Donald Trump will appear at Iowa Republican dinner in June

THOMAS BEAUMONT TBEAUMONT@DMREG.COM © 2011, DES MOINES REGISTER AND TRIBUNE CO.
MARCH 23, 2011 ET

Donald Trump plans to make his first Iowa appearance as a presidential prospect on June 10 as the headline speaker for the Iowa Republican Party's Lincoln Day dinner, state GOP officials told The Des Moines Register Tuesday.Trump's Iowa appearance is in part the product of the state GOP chairman Matt Strawn's effort to maintain focus on Iowa, whose influence on the early nominating campaign is undergoing renewed scrutiny.

The June event also underscores how the state party is inviting would-be candidates for individual appearances, instead of the multicandidate cavalcades of previous years.Trump said in a Des Moines Register interview this month he expects to announce his plans in June.Top billing for the leadoff caucus state's premier spring GOP fundraiser is expected to lead speculation about the New York billionaire and reality TV star, just as word did last week when Trump announced plans for a June visit to New Hampshire the leadoff primary state.

Strawn said he approached Trump during a trip to New York last month, after seeing him speak to the Conservative Political Action Conference in Washington, D.C."When he decided to make a CPAC appearance and first started making rumblings of potentially exploring a presidential run, I thought, if that's the case, we need to reach out to him to headline one of our events," Strawn said in an interview.Strawn met with Trump and a top deputy, Michael Cohen, at Trump's Manhattan office on Feb. 22, the day before the Iowa GOP chairman appeared on MSNBC's morning cable news program to discuss early moves in the 2012 caucus campaign.

Trump committed during the meeting to the dinner, expected to be held in Des Moines. Although party officials had not yet announced a venue, they said it is expected to draw a crowd similar to the audience of more than 1,000 that turned out to hear former Alaska Gov. Sarah Palin at the Iowa GOP's fall dinner in Des Moines last September.Trump told the Register he planned to campaign aggressively in Iowa if he seeks the 2012 nomination. The June 10 event comes just two months before the Ames straw poll, a party fundraiser at Iowa State University that also tests candidates' ability to turn out supporters.

The week after Strawn met with Trump and Cohen, Cohen visited Iowa to meet with Republican leaders. Cohen is co-founder of a website aimed at gauging support for a Trump candidacy.Trump plans to have announced his plans before attending the June 10 event, Cohen told the Register Tuesday."Either he will be the keynote speaker as a candidate at the dinner or he will just be an honored guest," Cohen said in a telephone interview. "He's not going to make an announcement at the event. He will be announcing his plans before that."

The banquet highlights the different approach the Iowa GOP is taking to the 2012 campaign from four years ago. In April 2007, 10 Republican presidential prospects paraded across the stage at the Polk County Convention Complex, giving short speeches to the audience of activists.This year, Strawn has opted to hold events around the state featuring individual presidential prospects. Mississippi Gov. Haley Barbour attended the first one last week in Davenport.

The shift was aimed in part at taking the focus off Des Moines and shifting it to county-level party organizations, plus drawing more media attention than a single event would.However, the party also has offered its bigger stages since the 2008 election to many presidential prospects, and offered invitations to others.Those who have headlined bigger state GOP events besides the chairman's new series include Barbour, former Minnesota Gov. Tim Pawlenty, former Massachusetts Gov. Mitt Romney, former U.S. House Speaker Newt Gingrich, Rep. Ron Paul and former U.S. Sen. Rick Santorum.

"I think quite frankly it's more fair to the keynote speakers when they get the stage to themselves," Strawn said."The campaigns really appreciate that approach because they're not just one of eight people who get seven minutes."

- <u>Home</u>
- <u>About Donald Trump</u>
- <u>Get Involved</u>
- <u>Your Voices...</u>
    - o <u>More Voices</u>
- <u>On YouTube</u>
- <u>Latest News</u>
- <u>Media</u>
- <u>Contact Us</u>

<u>Should Donald Trump Run For President?</u>

Are you one of the many frustrated Americans sick and tired of hearing the same old mundane political campaign promises? Empty promises echo across the nation every four years; stringing us along as we wait for something good to finally happen. Well it is finally here, and it is real. It is DONALD J. TRUMP. We need to convince Donald Trump to run for President in 2012 and end all of the old rhetoric occurring in Washington. This campaign will sweep a nation ready for "real" change and improve the lives of each and every American citizen. Trump has the knowledge, the resources, the power and the experience needed to re-shape our ailing nation; restoring our hope. Under his guidance, The United States of America will once again be the land of opportunity, prosperity and strength! [click to continue...]

<u>Trump May Run as Independent if GOP Picks 'Loser'</u>

SEAN HANNITY, HOST: Billionaire Donald Trump was at one time the leading candidate to challenge President Barack Obama in 2012. But now that he's decided to continue his television series "The Celebrity Apprentice," his presidential ambitions are on hold at least for the time being.

Now earlier today, I visited him at his Trump Tower offices in New York to talk about the possibility that he could make a surprise entrance into the 2012 race as an independent and much more.

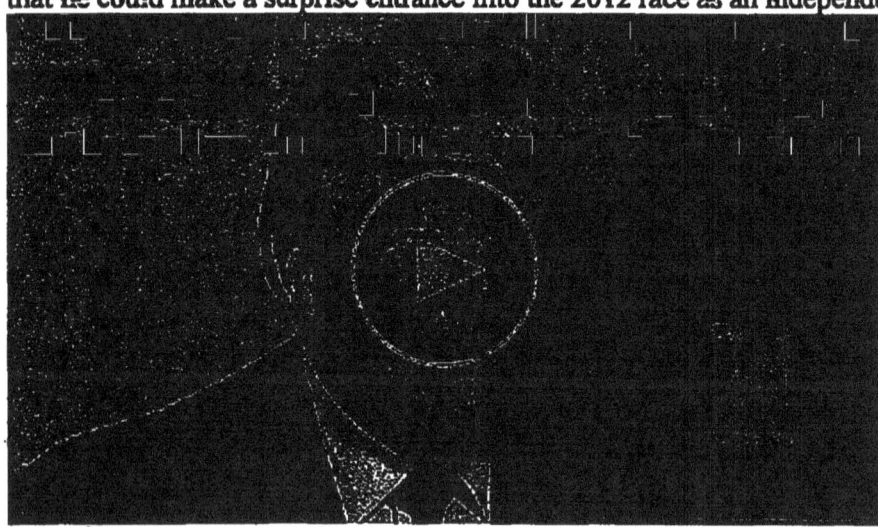

Happy Birthday Donald Trump!

Donald Tump turns 65. today! Congratulations and happy birthday, Mr. Trump!

Submit your birthday wishes in the comments below...

From Donald Trump...

"Thanks for all of your tremendous support over the past few months, stay tuned!"

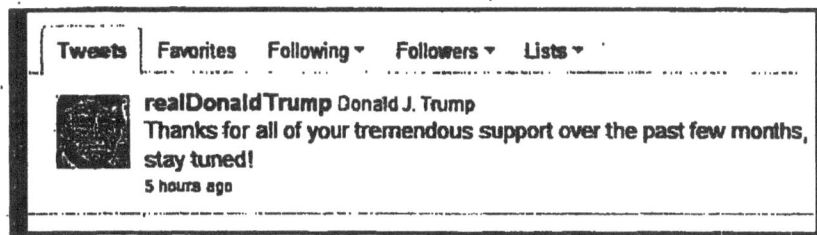

Vote for Trump in Bill O'Reilly's Poll Now

Fox news host Bill O'Rielly is running a poll – Donal Trump Vs. Mitt Romney. Show your support by voting for Donald Trump! Tell your friends and neighbors, share this link! Vote for Donald Trump Here!

Read the full article

Franklin Graham: Trump Might be Candidate of Choice

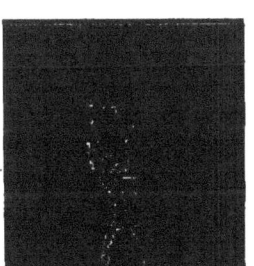

The Rev. Franklin Graham, whose family has served as spiritual advisers to numerous prominent political figures, told "This Week" anchor Christiane Amanpour that businessman Donald Trump might be his candidate of choice in 2012 and that he does not think former Alaska Gov. Sarah Palin will run for president.

Read the full article

Video: Thank You Mr. Donald Trump

Dr. James David Manning thanks Donald Trump for his efforts. Recorded on 27 April 2011. For More Info Go To: http://atlahmedianetwork.org or http://atlah.org.

Read the full article

Act Now!

Read the full article

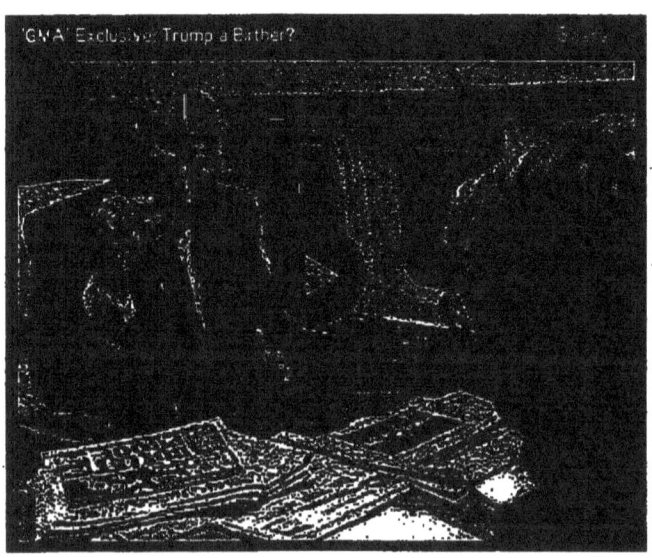

- **Should Trump Run? (Poll Closed)**

    Should Donald Trump enter the 2012 presidential race?

Yes (67%, 19,584 Votes)

No (33%, 9,522 Votes)

Total Voters: **29,095**

- **Trump Vs. Obama**

    Who would you favor in the 2012 Presidential Election?

    O Donald J. Trump
    O Barack Obama

<u>View Results</u>

- **How Would You Vote? (Poll Closed)**

    Would you vote for Donald Trump in 2012?

Attachment __2__
Page __4__ of __6__

Yes (66%, 19,562 Votes)

No (34%, 10,005 Votes)

Total Voters: **29,567**

- **Latest News:**

Video: Donald Trump goes on the record about creating jobs.

Watch video interview here...

Attachment 2
Page 5 of 6

This site is owned and operated by Gotham Government Relations and Communications | Sitemap
This site is not endorsed by Donald J. Trump

11473734

Form **8871**

(Rev. July 2003)

Department of the Treasury
Internal Revenue Service

Political Organization
Notice of Section 527 Status

OMB No. 1545-1693

Part I General Information

1 Name of organization
Should Trump Run Committee, Inc.

Employer Identification number
45 - 3145579

2 Mailing address (P.O. box or number, street, and room or suite number)
650 Town Center Drive Suite 1200

City or town, state, and ZIP code
Costa Mesa, CA 92626

3 Check applicable box: ✓ Initial notice   __ Amended notice   __ Final notice

4a Date established
09/01/2011

4b Date of material change

5 E-mail address of organization
no@email

6a Name of custodian of records
Pamela Jensen

6b Custodian's address
650 Town Center Drive Suite 1200
Costa Mesa, CA 92626

7a Name of contact person
Pamela Jensen

7b Contact person's address
650 Town Center Drive Suite 1200
Costa Mesa, CA 92626

8 Business address of organization (if different from mailing address shown above). Number, street, and room or suite number
650 Town Center Drive Suite 1200

City or town, state, and ZIP code
Costa Mesa, CA 92626

9a Election authority

9b Election authority identification number

NONE

Part II Notification of Claim of Exemption From Filing Certain Forms (see instructions)

10a Is this organization claiming exemption from filing Form 8872, Political Organization Report of Contributions and Expenditures, as a qualified state or local political organization? Yes __ No ✓

10b If 'Yes,' list the state where the organization files reports:

11 Is this organization claiming exemption from filing Form 990 (or 990-EZ), Return of Organization Exempt from Income Tax, as a caucus or association of state or local officials? Yes __ No ✓

Part III Purpose

12 Describe the purpose of the organization

To explore the possibility/determine support and solicit funds to draft Donald J. Trump to run for President of the United States.

Part IV List of All Related Entities (see instructions)

13 Check if the organization has no related entities.. ✓

14a Name of related entity	14b Relationship	14c Address

Part V List of All Officers, Directors, and Highly Compensated Employees (see instructions)

15a Name	15b Title	15c Address
Michael D. Cohen	President	650 Town Center Drive Suite 1200 Costa Mesa, CA 92626
Pamela Jensen	Secretary/Treasurer	650 Town Center Drive Suite 1200 Costa Mesa, CA 92626

Under penalties of perjury, I declare that the organization named in Part I is to be treated as a tax-exempt organization described in section 527 of the Internal Revenue Code, and that I have examined this notice, including accompanying schedules and statements, and to the best of my knowledge and belief, it is true, correct, and complete. I further declare that I am the official authorized to sign this report, and I am signing by entering my name below.

Pamela Jensen   09/01/2011

Sign Here ▶ _____ ▶ _____
Name of authorized official   Date

We need your help to get Donald Trump to Run!

1. Fill out the form below to "Join the Movement".

2. Send an email to Mr. Trump!

Join the Movement & Lets Get Trump to Run!

First Name: *

Last Name:

Email: *

Address:

City:

State:

- None -

Zip Code: *

Phone:

example - 2125551212

Cell Number For Alerts:

Get Exclusive Text Alerts - Enter Phone in the following format: 2125551212

Twitter:

Volunteer:

○ yes

○ no

Get Email Updates:

yes

┌─ CAPTCHA ──────────────────────────────────
│ This question is for testing whether you are a human visitor and to
│ prevent automated spam submissions.
│
│ **Math question:** *
│ 2 + 0 = [   ]
│ Solve this simple math problem and enter the result. E.g. for 1+3, enter 4.
└──

Sign Up Now

Recent blog posts

Donald Trump 'On the Record'
Pro-Donald Trump Website Evolves Into 527 Group
Donald Trump Answers Boy's Prayer for New Bike
The Eric Trump Foundation
From The Desk Of Donald Trump: Hurricane Irene and Libya
Video Pick: Donald Trump - Beyond the Boardroom with Jonathan Tisch
Trump: Debt Super Committee is 'Ridiculous'
Country Needs Third Party President
Trump: 'Obama's Constantly on Vacation'
Donald Trump Handicaps the 2012 Republican Field
more

Recent comments

For Such A Time As This
13 hours 39 min ago
BABY BOOMERS ARE HEADED TOWARDS THE WOODS
2 days 12 hours ago
TRUMP IS RIGHT AGAIN lawmakers target China with currency bill
2 days 19 hours ago
Report: Trade deficit with China cost Maine 9,545 Jobs
3 days 14 hours ago
Please, please be our President!
3 days 19 hours ago
THE REPUBLICAN PLATFORM OF 1872 READS LIKE A TRUMP SPEECH
4 days 21 hours ago
Eric
6 days 21 hours ago
THE REPUBLICAN PARTY IS STARTING TO LISTEN TO TRUMP
6 days 22 hours ago
I AM CHINESE AND I SUPPORT DONALD TRUMP FOR PRESIDENT NOW
1 week 17 hours ago
THE CHINESE JUST MADE A TACTICAL ERROR
1 week 1 day ago

 Should Donald Trump Run For President in 2012?

Like

 Should Donald Trump Run For President in 2012? shared a link.

 **Merrick Civic Association Discuss Trump on the Oce**
jonesbeachalliance.org
Rafe Lieber spoke on behalf of the Alliance for the Revital
Many residents are concerned about the Trump on the Oc
affect the Jones Beach waterfront.

September 22 at 1:46pm

 Should Donald Trump Run For President in 2012? shared a link.

Screw China, says Donald Trump
smh.com.au   news.smh.com.au
Screw China, says Donald Trump

September 21 at 11:27am

Should Donald Trump Run For President?

Fri, 2011-01-21 09:05 | ShouldTrumpRun

Are you one of the many frustrated Americans sick and tired of hearing the same old mundane political campaign promises? Empty promises echo across the nation every four years; stringing us along as we wait for something good to finally happen. Well it is finally here, and it is real. It is DONALD J. TRUMP. We need to convince Donald Trump to run for President in 2012 and end all of the old rhetoric occurring in Washington. This campaign will sweep a nation ready for "real" change and improve the lives of each and every American citizen.

Trump has the knowledge, the resources, the power and the experience needed to re-shape our ailing nation; restoring our hope. Under his guidance, The United States of America will once again be the land of opportunity, prosperity and strength!

Join me in creating a grass roots movement designed to save the greatest democracy in the world. Our country is heading down a dangerous path. I ask you to help me urge Donald Trump to throw his hat into the political ring. Our elected officials are mortgaging away our future by spending money that we do not have and in the process, creating unsustainable deficits.

We need to stop the bleeding now and Donald Trump will help to heal our economic wounds. We cannot afford to allow foreign countries to take advantage of us, improve their economies and leave our citizens without jobs. Donald Trump will even out the playing field and develop a legitimate plan to reign in our massive trade deficits.

Vote Now And Join The Movement!

ShouldTrumpRun's blog | Comments | Tags: Latest News

Donald Trump 'On the Record'

Fri, 2011-09-16 01:46 | admin

admin's blog | Add new comment | Comments | Tags: Latest News,
Video Picks

Pro-Donald Trump Website Evolves Into 527 Group

Fri, 2011-09-02 11:44 | admin

ABC's Michael Falcone and Jennifer Wlach report:

Read more
admin's blog | 10 comments | Comments | Tags: Latest News

Donald Trump Answers Boy's Prayer for New Bike

Tue, 2011-08-30 00:25 | admin

After his bike was stolen out of his parents' garage, 10-year-old Culley
Larson posted a video to YouTube praying to get it back. Thanks to
Donald Trump, Larson's prayers were answered. After seeing Larson's
video on Fox New Channel, Trump bought Larson a brand new bike,
which he gave to him on Fox and Friends this morning.
admin's blog | 2 comments | Comments | Tags: Video Picks

The Eric Trump Foundation

Sat, 2011-08-27 19:57 | admin

The Eric Trump Foundation strives to improve the lives of children battling
life-threatening diseases at St. Jude Children's Research Hospital. What
began as the collaborative effort of Eric Trump and several friends five
years ago has grown to include over 300(+) donors and world-class
sponsors. To date, we have raised over $3 million to support children and
families in need.

www.erictrumpfoundation.com
admin's blog | 1 comment | Comments | Tags: Video Picks

From The Desk Of Donald Trump:
Hurricane Irene and Libya

Sat, 2011-08-27 19:52 | admin

admin's blog | 2 comments | Comments | Tags: Video Picks

Video Pick: Donald Trump - Beyond
the Boardroom with Jonathan Tisch

Tue, 2011-08-23 14:23 | admin

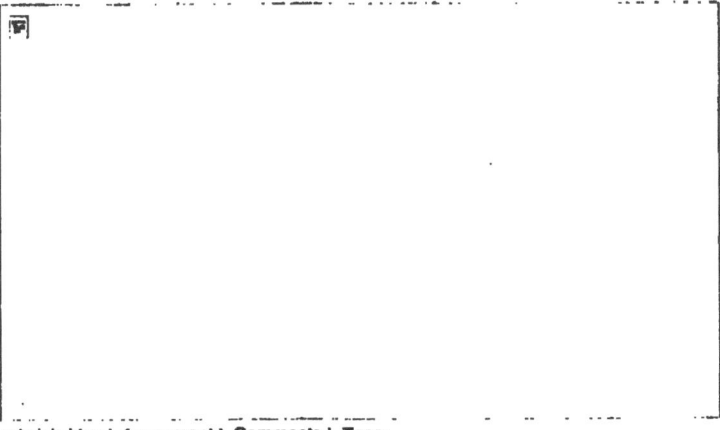

admin's blog | 1 comment | Comments | Tags:

Trump: Debt Super Committee Is 'Ridiculous'

Tue, 2011-08-23 14:03 | admin

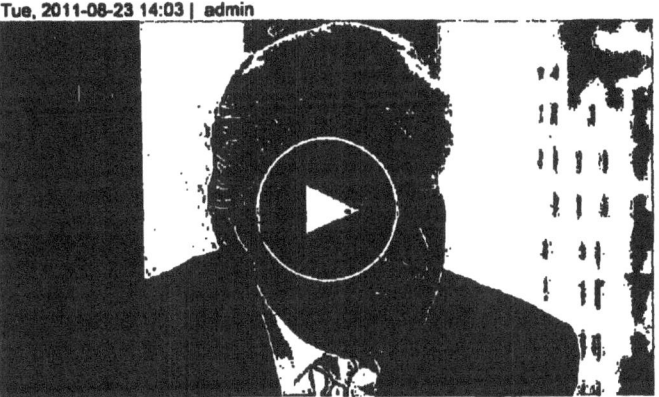

admin's blog | Add new comment | Comments | Tags: Debt Ceiling

Country Needs Third Party President

Sat, 2011-08-20 10:26 | admin

Friday, August 19, 2011 10:07 AM   Read more

admin's blog | 6 comments | Comments | Tags: Uncategorized

Trump: 'Obama's Constantly on Vacation'

Fri, 2011-08-19 12:12 | admin

admin's blog | 6 comments | Comments | Tags: Budget, Economy & Free Markets, Video Picks

1 2 next › last »

Piryx™

- Share This Page

- Like 82

- Tweet 0

- 0

Donate to Should Trump Run

http://www.ShouldTrumpRun.com

Please consider giving a donation to Should Trump Run Committe, INC. Our goal is to encourage Mr. Trump –who is NOT presently a candidate—to become one, and to explore the potential support for his possible candidacy. We are doing this effort 100% grassroots and are relying on individual donors and volunteers.

We respect your privacy. Your contact information is secure and not sold or given to third parties. Let's start taking America back to number one!

Contributions may also be made by check or money order, payable "Should Trump Run Committee" and mail to 650 Town Center Drive, 12th Floor, Costa Mesa, CA 92626. Click here to download form to mail in.

Personal Information

- First NameRequired

- Middle Name

- Last NameRequired

- EmailRequired

- Home AddressRequired

- Home Address (line 2)

- CityRequired

- StateRequired

- Zip/PostalRequired

- Home PhoneRequired

- Work Phone

- Fax Phone

- Mobile Phone

Employment Information

- EmployerRequired

- OccupationRequired

-

Contribution Amount

- ⌀
  $25
- ⌀
  $50
- ⌀
  $100
- ⌀
  $250
-

- ⌀
  $500
- ⌀
  $1,000
- ⌀
  $2,500
- ⌀
  $[   ]
-

Sharing Is Caring

Like   82 people like this.

Payment Information

- ⦿ E-Check
- ⌀ Visa
- ⌀ Mastercard
- ⌀ Amex
- ⌀ Discover

- Routing Number

- Account Number

  ⑈125598589   ⑆02   125469 87⑈

  [ROUTING NUMBER (9 DIGITS)]   [ACCOUNT NUMBER]

Billing Information

- ⎕ Same as home address.
- Billing Address

- Billing Address (line 2)

- City

- State
  [▾]

- Zip/Postal

Contribution Type

- ○ I want to donate the above amount a single time.
- ○ I want to donate the above amount today and continue donating monthly for [every month until cancelled ▼] starting October 22.

Legal Compliance

☐ ffirm that the following statements are true and accurate:

1) I am a United States citizen or lawfully admitted for permanent residence (e.g., "green card holder")
2) This is my personal credit card and the contribution is made using my personal funds
3) This contribution is not made using a business credit card or from the general treasury funds of a corporation, labor union, national bank, or an entity that is a federal government contractor
4) I will not be reimbursmi by any other individual or entity for this contribution
5) I agree that if Mr. Trump does run, the first $2,500 of my contribution shall then be designated for the 2012 general election. Any donation in excess of $2500 must either be refunded or redesignated to a spouse.
6) Donations are not deductible for federal income tax purposes.

☑ I want to publish my name to the Donate to Should Trump Run giving stream! (Note: your contribution amount will not be shown)

Submit

☐ piryx™

Piryx - The Social Giving Platform

New fundraising is as easy as writing a blog or posting a status update and can be integrated into your website, product or mobile app. With Piryx, causes raise money online in more volume and much more effectively across the web. To learn more and create your own free account visit Piryx.com.

To: SHOULD TRUMP RUN COMMITTEE, INC:

[   ] Yes, Mr. Trump SHOULD run for president. Please do all you can to encourage others to support Mr. Trump, and to urge him to run.

I enclose my maximum donation of:

[   ] $25   [   ] $50   [   ] $100   [   ] $250   [   ] $500   [   ] $1,000   [   ] $2,500   [   ] $_____

By completing the information, below, I certify that:

1) I am a United States citizen or lawfully admitted for permanent residence (e.g., "green card holder").
2) Any check enclosed is drawn on my personal account, and the contribution is made using my personal funds.
3) This contribution is not made using a business check, or from the general treasury funds of a corporation, labor union, national bank, or an entity that is a federal government contractor.
4) I will not be reimbursed by any other individual or entity for this contribution.
5) I agree that if Mr. Trump does run, the first $2,500 of my contribution shall then be designated for the 2012 general election. Any donation in excess of $2500 must either be refunded or redesignated to a spouse.
6) Donations are not deductible for federal income tax purposes.

My Name is:_____ (Required by federal law)

My occupation is: _____ (Required by federal law)

My employer is: _____ (Required by federal law)

My Street address is: _____ (Required by federal law)

_____ (Required by federal law)

My phone number is: _____

My email address is: _____

> Please mail this form, along with your check to:
> Should Trump Run Committee, Inc.
> Pamela Jensen, Treasurer
> 650 Town Center Drive, 12th Floor
> Costa Mesa, CA 92626

Paid for by SHOULD TRUMP RUN COMMITTEE, INC.
Not authorized by any candidate or candidate's committee

www.TrumpHQ.com

HOME   DONALD TRUMP   JOIN THE MOVEMENT   YOUR VOICES   BLOG   CONTACT

1. Fill out the form below to "Join the Movement".

2. Send an email to Mr. Trump!

ADD MY SUPPORT

Welcome to TRUMP Headquarters!

TrumpHQ.com, formerly ShouldTrumpRun.com, is the new home for the Donald Trump supporters. Are you one of the many frustrated Americans sick and tired of hearing the same old mundane political campaign promises? Empty promises echo across the nation every four years; stringing us along as we wait for something good to finally happen. Well it is finally here, and it is real. It is DONALD J. TRUMP. We need to convince Donald Trump to go to Washington.

We fully respect Mr. Trump's decision to endorse Mitt Romney, but firmly believe that we need Trump in DC. Imagine Donald Trump as Secretary of State "negotiating" with the China or OPEC! Help us keep up the pressure and send Trump to DC. This campaign will sweep a nation ready for "real" change and improve the lives of each and every American citizen.

Trump has the knowledge, the resources, the power and the experience needed to re-shape our ailing nation; restoring our hope. Under his guidance, The United States of America will once again be the land of opportunity, prosperity and strength! Join me in creating a grass roots movement designed to save the greatest democracy in the world. Our country is heading down a dangerous path. I ask you to help me urge Donald Trump to throw his hat into the political ring.

Our elected officials are mortgaging away our future by spending money that we do not have and in the process, creating unsustainable deficits. We need to stop the bleeding now and Donald Trump will help to heal our economic wounds. We cannot afford to allow foreign countries to take advantage of us, improve their economies and leave our citizens without jobs. Donald Trump will even out the playing field and develop a legitimate plan to reign in our massive trade deficits.

Join the Movement & Lets Get Trump To DC!

First Name: *

Last Name:

Email: *

Address:

Poll

Donald Trump would be the best:

○ President

○ Vice President

○ Secretary of State

○ Secretary of Defense

○ Secretary of Commerce

Vote

Recent blog posts

TRUMPHQ.com - New Website

Action Alerts: Trump: It's Time to Get Tough

Trump Threatens to Spend Millions on a Presidential Run

From The Desk Of Donald Trump: Iran and Occupy Wall Street

Trump on Fox and Friends - Should Trump Endorse?

http://www.shouldtrumprun.com/

City: _____

State:
- None -   [▼]

Zip Code: *
_____

Phone:
_____
example - 2125551212

Cell Number For Alerts:
_____
Get Exclusive Text Alerts - Enter Phone in the following format: 2125551212

Twitter:
_____

Volunteer:

○ yes

○ no

Get Email Updates:
[yes ▼]

┌─CAPTCHA───
│ This question is for testing whether you are a human visitor and to prevent automated spam submissions.
│
│ Math question: *
│ 1 + 5 = [   ]
│ Solve this simple math problem and enter the result. E.g. for 1+3, enter 4.
└──

Sign Up Now

┌──
│ Find us on Facebook
│
│ [Sign Up]   Create an account or log in to see what your friends like.
│
│   Should Donald Trump Run For President in 2012?
│   Like
│
│   Should Donald Trump Run For President In 2012?
│   Do you watch "The Apprentice"? Who should be fired?
│
│   Celebrity Apprentice Recap: Which Celeb Wocka-Walked Away From the
│   Boardroom Empty Handed? - E! Onl
│   www.eonline.com
│   Find out which celebrity Donald Trump sent sent home in this week's episode
│
│   April 15 at 9:50pm
│
│   Should Donald Trump Run For President in 2012?
│   What do you think?
│   George Zimmerman to be charged in Trayvon Martin shooting
│
│ Facebook social plugin
└──

From The Desk Of
Donald Trump: Jon
Stewart
Is Trump a Kingmaker
in 2012 Race?
Donald Trump 'On the
Record'
Pro-Donald Trump
Website Evolves Into
527 Group
Donald Trump Answers
Boy's Prayer for New
Bike
                    more

IT'S COLD OUTSIDE...
SO WHERE'S
THE GLOBAL
WARMING?
- DONALD J. TRUMP

User login

Username: *
_____

Password: *
_____

Log in
Request new password

www.TrumpHQ.com

HOME   DONALD TRUMP   JOIN THE MOVEMENT   YOUR VOICES   BLOG   CONTACT

Home | Blogs | admin's blog

TRUMPHQ.com - New Website

Mon, 2012-03-26 22:31 | admin

TrumpHQ.com, formerly ShouldTrumpRun.com is the new home for the Trump supporters. Are you one of the many frustrated Americans sick and tired of hearing the same old mundane political campaign promises? Empty promises echo across the nation every four years; stringing us along as we wait for something good to finally happen. Well it is finally here, and it is real. It is DONALD J. TRUMP.

We need to convince Donald Trump to go to Washington. We fully respect Mr. Trump's decision to endorse Mitt Romney, but firmly believe that we need Trump in DC. Imagine Donald Trump as Secretary of State "negotiating" with the China or OPEC! Help us keep up the pressure and send Trump to DC. This campaign will sweep a nation ready for "real" change and improve the lives of each and every American citizen.

admin's blog | Login to post comments | Tags: Uncategorized

Poll

Donald Trump would be the best:

○ President

○ Vice President

○ Secretary of State

○ Secretary of Defense

○ Secretary of Commerce

Vote

Recent blog posts

TRUMPHQ.com - New Website

Action Alerts: Trump: It's Time to Get Tough

Trump Threatens to Spend Millions on a Presidential Run

From The Desk Of Donald Trump: Iran and Occupy Wall Street

Trump on Fox and Friends - Should Trump Endorse?

From The Desk Of Donald Trump: Jon Stewart

Is Trump a Kingmaker in 2012 Race?

Donald Trump 'On the Record'

Pro-Donald Trump Website Evolves Into 527 Group

Donald Trump Answers Boy's Prayer for New Bike

more

User login

Username: *

Password: *

Log in

Request new password

TrumpHQ.com is not associated with Donald J. Trump
Not authorized by any candidate or candidate's committee.
©2011 TrumpHQ.com

www.ingramcontent.com/pod-product-compliance
Lightning Source LLC
Chambersburg PA
CBHW081758280526
45789CB00008B/2909